MW01140126

Prank *and* Pray You Get Away!

Over 60 Fun Jokes to Play on Your Sibling

William Eshleman
with Paige Kimball

Original Edition

Find Your Way Publishing, Inc.
PO BOX 667
Norway, Maine

Prank and Pray You Get Away!
Over 60 Fun Jokes to Play on Your Sibling

Copyright © 2012
by William Eshleman and Paige Kimball

Published by:
Find Your Way Publishing, Inc.
PO BOX 667
Norway, ME 04268 U.S.A.
www.findyourwaypublishing.com

Library of Congress Control Number: 2012931820
ISBN-13: 978-0-9849322-0-7
ISBN-10: 0-9849322-0-8
1st Edition, 2012
Printed in the United States of America

Dedication

This book is dedicated to our brother, Wyatt because without him we wouldn't have been able to write it. We love you very much Wyatt!

And also to our sister, Marrae, who taught us a lot of these. We love you too Marrae!

To our family and friends who are always supportive.

To all families and siblings out there who honor family no matter how you define it. Biological, adoptive, half, step, friends, etc. It doesn't matter how you define it, "family" is family!

And last but not least, to all of the men and women who serve in the military and fight for our freedom.

Thank you!!!

Acknowledgments

We would like to thank everyone involved in helping us write this book. This includes our brother, Wyatt and our sister, Marrae, along with our parents, Ed and Melissa Eshleman. We had many family meetings and brainstorming sessions around the dinner table that were always very helpful. Our siblings also put up with us testing these jokes out on them and our parents had to listen to it, and for that we thank them!

Although the title of this book is used in a fun and playful manner, we do believe in the power of prayer and would like to thank God, the Divine Source for all of the blessings in our lives and for all that is.

We would also like to acknowledge everyone who is making a positive difference. Let's lighten up, have fun, & laugh more!

"Siblings are the people we practice on, the people who teach us about fairness and cooperation and kindness and caring quite often the hard way."

~ *Pamela Dugdale*

About This Book

We have tested all of the ideas in this book and we assure you that they work. Having said that, this book is given to you to help you grow closer to your sibling by joking with them in loving ways. And to create enjoyable memories that will last a lifetime.

This book should be used as a tool to grow your relationship with fun and humor. You don't always need to be sensitive and mushy to establish a stronger bond with your sibling.

Have fun, and the goal is not to make your sibling mad, but to create wonderful memories that will bring you closer together. If your sibling starts to get really annoyed, back off and try again another day when he or she is in a better mood. And remember if you make a mess taking any of our advice, clean it up. The goal is to have fun and laugh together!

Contents

"A friend is a brother who was once a bother."

~ *Unknown*

1. Nicknames

This is one of the funniest ways to joke with your sibling. Give him nicknames that he doesn't like. A few examples are: Figgy, Bigfooty, Fartypants, Sweetlips. Pick one and refer to him with this name in the nicest, sweetest voice possible. And do it often.

"Our brothers and sisters are there with us from the dawn of our personal stories to the inevitable dusk."

~ *Susan Scarf Merrell*

2. Sing!

Sing really loud and annoying near your sibling.

Sing nursery rhymes over and over. Some ideas are "Row, row, row your boat", "Twinkle, twinkle little star", or "Mary had a little lamb". You could even sing the Barney song.

When her favorite songs come on, sing them loud but mess up all the words.

Practice all of these while acting like you are being sincere. Pretend like you are trying your best.

"Brothers and sisters are as close as hands and feet."

~ *Vietnamese Proverb*

3.   Jump!

Jump on his bed whenever you get the chance. Even when he is in it! When he's not in it, jump on it while he is doing something else in his room. Mess up all of his blankets and bedding.

(Remember if you mess up his bed, the polite thing to do is fix it or remake it. This will only take a few minutes but will be worth it!)

"I, who have no sisters or brothers, look with some degree of innocent envy on those who may be said to be born to friends."

~ *James Boswell*

 **4. Wet willy**

Wet willies can be so annoying and gross! When your sibling is least expecting it, lick and wet your finger, then gently wiggle it into his or her ear.

"I don't believe an accident of birth makes people sisters or brothers. It makes them siblings, gives them mutuality of parentage. Sisterhood and brotherhood is a condition people have to work at."

~ *Maya Angelou*

5. Boo!

Scare your sibling every chance you get. Stand behind a door, or behind the shower curtain. Hide under her bed and grab her leg. Hide in a closet that you know she is going to get into. Hide under a blanket in the corner of the room. The options are unlimited!

"A brother shares childhood memories and grown-up dreams."

~ *Unknown*

6. Take, then return

Take stuff from your sibling's room and when he or she asks where it is, pretend that, not only do you not know where their stuff is, but that you have no idea what they are even talking about!

(Only do this for a few minutes and then give back the item. We like to tell our siblings that they should thank us for "finding" it.)

"If you want to know how your girl will treat you after marriage, just listen to her talking to her little brother."

~ *Sam Levenson*

7. Flatulence

Sit on your sibling and fart. Fart in his room and walk out. Or fart and then blame the stench on him (this is especially funny if his girlfriend is visiting).

"I am smiling because you are my brother. I am laughing because there is nothing you can do about it!"

~ *Unknown*

8. Make fun

Make fun of your sibling by questioning her choice of clothing, boyfriends (or girlfriends), question anything she does. Then when she tries to explain, sarcastically agree with her by saying "Ohhhh okay, whatever you say."

"To the outside world, we all grow old. But not to brothers and sisters. We know each other as we always were. We know each other's hearts. We share private family jokes. We remember family feuds and secrets, family griefs and joys. We live outside the touch of time."

~ *Clara Ortega*

9.   Photo shot

This one is a lot of fun. When your sibling isn't around, take photos of yourself in his room with all of his favorite things and then post them. For example, take a photo of yourself wearing his favorite hat, shirt, jacket, sunglasses, etc. then post the photo on your facebook or myspace profile. Do this several times with different things over long periods of time to make it more effective!

"A brother is a friend given by Nature."

~ *Jean Baptiste Legouve*

10. Wake up call

Wake your sibling up really early on the weekend and tell her that it's time to get ready for school. When she's wide awake and realizes it's not a school day apologize and tell her you were just trying to be helpful. Do the same thing the following weekend and so on.

"Lord help the mister that comes
between me and my sister..."
~ *Irving Berlin*

11. Squirt bottle

Squirt bottles are so much fun! Here's what we do. Our cat likes to get on the kitchen counters and table; therefore, we always have a squirt bottle readily available. We pretend to squirt the cat but purposefully miss her and squirt our brother instead when he least expects it. Then we say "Whoops, we were way off, sorry about that!"

If you don't have an excuse like a cat for a squirt bottle, you should get one just the same. You can use it to defend yourself anytime your sibling comes at you for pestering him!

"It snowed last year too: I made a
    snowman and my brother
    knocked it down and I knocked
    my brother down and then we
    had tea."

                    ~ *Dylan Thomas*

12. Freezer

The freezer is great for a lot of things including taking your brothers underwear, wetting them with water, and then freezing them. When your brother goes to get ice-cream he will see his frozen underwear! You can also freeze a couple pairs of his underwear and put them back in his draw the next morning before he wakes up or while he is in the shower.

(Be sure to put a plastic bag under the frozen underwear in his draw so that everything else in the draw doesn't get wet as they thaw out.)

There's no other love like the love for a brother. There's no other love like the love from a brother."

~ *Terri Guillemets*

 **13. T.P.**

You guessed it! T.P. stands for toilet paper. Get a roll of toilet paper and unravel it all over your sibling's room or if you share a room, unravel it all over HER side of the room! She will be very surprised and annoyed when she walks in and sees that her bedroom has been toilet papered.

(Remember the polite thing to do is help with the clean up. But again, it will totally worth it!)

"There is a little boy inside the man who is my brother... Oh, how I hated that little boy. And how I love him too."

~ *Anna Quindlan*

14. Slurp your peaches

Slurp your peaches or anything else for that matter! While sitting next to your sibling, slurp your peaches, soup, etc. Slurping your food is a fun way to pester your brother. When he asks you to stop, tell him you can't help slurping "slurpy" foods! And keep slurping!

"Siblings are there to provide you with love and support, but most importantly the truth."

~ *Unknown*

15. Hair

Mess up your sibling's hair when she isn't expecting it and tell her you're just trying to fix it for her.

If you have a brother and his hair is long enough, put clips or elastics in it while he is sleeping.

Another fun thing you can do with your brother's hair is get extreme hair spiking gel and put some in while he is sleeping. The colored gel is even better!

"I think I'm funny because my
family, my siblings were funny."
~ *Martin Short*

16. Wrong names

Call his friends by the wrong name. For example; if he has a friend named Nick, always refer to him as Josh. "So is Josh coming over this weekend?"

To REALLY pester him, call his girlfriends by the wrong names. If his girlfriend's name is Julie, keep referring to her as Julia, Karen are Carol, etc., etc.

(Remember only do this a few times. If your sibling seems to be really getting mad, then apologize and stop being a pest, for a little while anyway!)

"More than Santa Claus, your (sister or brother) knows when you've been bad or good."

~ *Linda Sunshine*

17. Annoying noises

The options for making annoying noises are unlimited. There are a million annoying noises you can make while in the presence of your sibling. The key is to keep making the noises. Tap your fingers on a table; use your tongue to make weird noises, make popping sounds with your gum, hum an annoying tune, etc.

"How do people make it through life without a (sister or brother)?"
~ *Sara Corpening*

18. Pillow

Put things under your sibling's pillow. Fake spiders, snakes, and insects work well for this. When they adjust their pillow before bed or reach under it in the middle of the night they will wonder what the heck it is and most likely jump out of their beds!

Or when you know he has a friend coming over place a Victoria Secrets catalog under his pillow with a corner of it sticking out. His friend will think he put it there. If you don't have a Victoria Secrets catalog, use your imagination. You can use a J.C.Penney or Sears flyer and cut out the sections you'd like.

"The mildest, drowsiest sister has been known to turn tiger if her sibling is in trouble."

~ *Clara Ortega*

19. Nonsense

When your sibling tries to tell you something, always respond with complete nonsense. Say something that makes no sense at all, for example if he tells you that he has homework respond with "boogily boo" or "pillow willow". You can also make up random responses. As long as it is nonsense, it will work!

"It was nice growing up with a brother - someone to lean on, someone to count on...someone to tell on!"

~ *Unknown*

20. Sweet dreams

There are several fun things you can do while your sibling is sleeping. You can take a washable marker and draw a pretty heart on his forehead. Or better yet, write "I love" with your name after it.

We've also heard of putting whip cream in your brother's hand then lightly tickling his nose with something. He will automatically itch it and get whip cream all over his face. (To be nice, you should probably have a towel ready.)

"The highlight of my childhood was making my brother laugh so hard that food came out of his nose."

~ *Garrison Keillor*

21. Hang on

Whenever your brother gets up to leave a room, grab onto his ankle and hang on. Let him drag you around a bit. Tell him you'd like a ride to the next room please.

"A sister is a little bit of childhood
that can never be lost."

~ *Marion C. Garretty*

22. Long hugs

Hug your brother and don't let go. Tell him you just want him to know that you care. Extra long hugs will pester your brother like crazy! (But will create great, fun memories.)

"Sibling relationships ... outlast marriages, survive the death of parents, resurface after quarrels that would sink any friendship. They flourish in a thousand incarnations of closeness and distance, warmth, loyalty and distrust."

~ *Erica E. Goode*

23. Can't take my eyes off of you

Constantly staring at your sibling will drive her crazy. Stare at her and when she asks what you're doing, act like nothing and look away. Then start doing it again. You could say "Sorry, I thought you had something in your hair." Or "I am looking at the wall behind you." Or "Oh, I'm just thinking about something that happened at school today and didn't realize that I was staring at you." And continue making silly excuses.

"Never let an angry sister comb your hair. "

~ *Unknown*

24. Be a tattletale

Tell on your sibling for things he didn't do. If YOU get in trouble for making a mess, just say your brother did it. You can also intentionally make a mess and say your brother did it. (Just remember to let your parents in on your plan ahead of time or quickly tell them that you're just joking.)

When our parents ask us who left the cup, or plate, or snack, or mess in the living room, we like to say our brother did. Then when he denies it, we quickly accept responsibility and clean it up. But boy is it fun seeing his face!

"Both within the family and without, our sisters hold up our mirrors: our images of who we are and of who we can dare to become."

~ *Elizabeth Fishel*

25. Grammar

Pronounce words wrong, use incorrect grammar, and make up new words. You can also use words incorrectly in a sentence. Sometimes we will ask our brother "Are you cereal?!" Instead of "Are you serious?" Or say "I ain't not gonna do that." You can also act smart by using big words, but be sure to use them incorrectly, just for fun! Look up a word in the dictionary and use it how you want.

"Brothers don't necessarily have to say anything to each other-they can sit in a room and be together and just be completely comfortable with each other."

~ *Leonardo DiCaprio*

26. He started it

Intentionally start little fights with your sibling and whenever your parents tell you to stop, always proclaim "But he started it!"

"Sisters annoy, interfere, criticize. Indulge in monumental sulks, in huffs, in snide remarks. Borrow. Break. Monopolize the bathroom. Are always underfoot. But if catastrophe should strike, sisters are there. Defending you against all corners."

~ *Pam Brown*

27. Front and center

When your sibling is watching television or playing video games, get in front of the TV. Then act as if you don't realize you are doing it. When she asks you to move, apologize, wait a few minutes, and do it again.

"Half the time when brothers wrestle, it's just an excuse to hug each other."

~ *James Patterson*

28. Powerless

Threaten your sibling with things you both know you are powerless to do. Tell him that if he doesn't do YOUR laundry, you WILL ground him. Or if he doesn't clean your room you will make him stack wood, take his cell phone privileges away, etc.

"Of all the things I have to play, I'd choose my brother any day."

~ *Unknown*

29. Whisper sweet nothings

While sitting next to your sibling, whisper sweet nothings in her ear; tell her that she is the best sister ever. Breathe and blow in her ear while you're at it. Then to top it off, burp in her ear and act like it was a mistake. You'll both know it wasn't and it will be a good laugh.

"Sisters don't need words. They have perfected a language of snarls and smiles and frowns and winks - expressions of shocked surprise and incredulity and disbelief. Sniffs and snorts and gasps and sighs - that can undermine any tale you're telling."

~ *Pam Brown*

30. Crackers

Crackers are wonderful for making a mess. Saltines work great. Snack on some crackers while sitting near your sibling and let the crumbs go everywhere. You should also talk to your sibling while eating the crackers; amazingly the cracker crumbs will fly right out of your mouth towards your brother. It will gross him out and totally annoy him!

(Remember to pick up your mess, but only *after* you've pestered your sibling.)

"My Brother, My Friend I love my
brother, my brother loves me.
My friend, my hero, he always
will be. In sundry ways our
uniqueness is clear. He likes to
go far, but I favor near. He likes
to play sports and being outside.
I prefer play music and playing
inside. Sometimes we fight and
scream at each other, but he is
my friend for he is my brother."
~ *Michele' Cobb*

31. Bubble gum

Get some bubble gum and chomp on it as loud and as long as you can in the presence of your sibling. You can also blow bubbles and pop them close to her face.

"Sweet is the voice of a sister in the season of sorrow."

~Benjamin Disraeli

32. Grapes

Put a grape in each of your brother's socks. He will get a slimy surprise when he puts them on. The green grapes won't stain as bad as the red grapes.

(This is easy to clean up. Just turn the socks inside out and wipe out with a paper towel. Easy as that!)

To the outside world, we all grow old. But not to brothers and sisters. We know each other as we always were. We know each other's hearts. We share private family jokes. We remember family feuds and secrets, family griefs and joys. We live outside the touch of time.

~*Clara Ortega*

33. Can't hear you

Ignore your sibling, especially when she is telling you to do something. If she asks you to do something, pretend you don't hear her. Ignore everything she says. (Do this at least for a few minutes anyway!)

"The bond of a brother and sister is stronger than any one could know with you in my life and with me by your side there's one thing that i know we will never have to fight one single battle alone."

~ *Unknown*

34. Knock, knock

Make up knock knock jokes that do not make sense.

> Knock knock
> Who's there?
> Mouse
> Mouse who?
> The mouse ran up the light bulb to catch the flower pot.

Then laugh like crazy and tell another.

"If thy brother wrongs thee, remember not so much his wrong-doing, but more than ever that he is thy brother."

~ *Epictetus*

35. Blow kisses

Every time your sibling looks your way, blow him a kiss and say "I love you bro". Blow him a kiss at the dinner table, while watching television, while playing videogames, or basketball. If you are brave, blow him a kiss in public.

"No one knows better than a sister
    or brother how we grew up, and
    who our friends, teachers and
    favorite toys were. No one
    knows better than they."
                                    ~ *Unknown*

36. Lock down

Make an excuse for your sibling to go outside then lock him out, just for a few minutes. Just long enough to be a pest. If possible, do this a few times a week.

"In the cookies of life, brothers and sisters are the chocolate chips."

~ *Unknown*

37. Dresses

Stock up your brother's bureau with a few dresses. Borrow a few dresses or sequined tank tops from your mom or sister's closet and put them on the very top of his clothes, so when he opens his draws all he will see are beautiful dresses.

Remember you will need to put all of your mom's or sister's clothes back as neatly as you found them! But yet again, it will be so worth it!

"It takes two men to make one brother."

~ *Israel Zangwill*

38. Paint

Paint your sibling's fingernails or toenails while they sleep. The brighter the colors the fingernail polish is the better. Craft paints work good for this because it will wash off easily. For a more subtle result, yet still just as funny, use clear coat fingernail polish.

(If you use fingernail polish you should probably do it on a weekend and make sure there is fingernail polish remover in the house.)

"Your brother or sister is your mirror, shining back at you with a world of possibilities. (She or He) is your witness, who sees you at your worst and best, and loves you anyway. (She or He) is your partner in crime, your midnight companion, someone who knows when you are smiling, even in the dark. (She or He) is your teacher, your defense attorney, your personal press agent, even your shrink. And some days, (she or he) is the reason you wish you were an only child."

~ *Barbara Alpert*

39. Copycat

This is obvious, siblings have been doing it forever, and it is one of the most annoying things ever.

Copy everything your sibling does! And have fun! But remember to stop if they appear to be getting mad. Just try again another time.

"I sought my soul, but my soul I could not see. I sought my God, but my God eluded me. I sought my brother and I found all three."

~ Unknown

40. Gum wrappers

Get a pack of gum and gently unwrap every single piece. Put the gum in a plastic bag so YOU can have it later. Refold all of the gum wrappers and carefully put the empty wrappers back into the pack. Put the package of gum in a place where your sibling will see it and get excited.

The nice thing to do is offer them a piece of the gum after they realize the entire pack is empty.

"I think people that have a brother or sister don't realize how lucky they are. Sure, they fight a lot, but to know that there's always somebody there, somebody that's family."

~ *Trey Parker*

41. Redecorate

Help your sibling by rearranging his room for him. Move some of his things around. Would his bureau look better in the middle of the room? Would his lamp look better on the floor? Would that picture look better sideways? Should his shoes be paired with mix matches? Would his pillow look better at the foot of his bed? The possibilities are endless! Just help your brother out would ya?

"Brothers are fun, until they're not."

~ Unknown

42. Label maker

Get an inexpensive label maker and label all of your sibling's things like the teachers do in kindergarten classrooms. Label his sock draw, label his underwear draw however you choose; we like the phrase "pull-ups", and you can even label any spare change you find lying around. Stick a "penny" label on his pennies.

Tell him you are trying to help him get organized!

"I don't care how poor a man is; if he has family, he's rich."
~ *Dan Wilcox & Thad Mumford*

43. *Don't* keep your hands to yourself

This is self explanatory. Find excuses to bump or literally run into your sibling. Tell him there is a bug on his shirt or hat, and flick it off. When passing him to go into another room, pretend to lose your balance and fall into him a bit. Remember this is all in fun and you don't want anyone to get hurt. So gently bump, flick, or fall into him! But have fun!

"Families are like fudge... mostly
sweet with a few nuts."

~ *Unknown*

44. Bless me

Get a little water on both of your hands. Pull your head back a bit, as if you are going to sneeze. Pretend to sneeze big and while covering your nose, quickly shake your hands towards your sibling. She will think you are sneezing all over her. Then apologize and say "Bless me!"

"Brothers and sisters ensure that
you will never, ever be alone."
~ *Unknown*

45. Simon says

While chilling out in the same room as your brother or sister, out of the blue look at them and say "Simon says please get me a drink of water". Do this throughout the entire day or just every now and then. If you share a room, in the morning say "Simon says please make my bed". Or "Simon says please make me breakfast". Think big! "Simon says please do my chores for the week". You might not get any of these things but it's definitely worth a try! Like the saying goes, "If at first you don't succeed, try, try again." Simon says!

"Sometimes I wish I could go back to the days when I was six and my biggest problem was what kind of dress to put on my Barbie's or whether or not I had enough Lego's to build a fort."

~ *Unknown*

46. Cookies

Get a package of cookies (we like Oreos because of the resealable top). Empty the package. You can either share them with others or save them in another container for yourself. Get some small rocks and fill the empty cookie package until it weighs about the same as it did when it had cookies in it. Put the package in a place that your brother will surely see them.

To be nice, you should definitely share some cookies after. At least one anyway!

"Even though we appear to be sewn in a different pattern, we have a common thread that won't be broken-by people or years or distance."

~ *Unknown*

47. Sanitize

Get some sanitizing wipes and follow your sibling around and sanitize everything they touch, in a quick-like manner like it's very important that you clean their germs off right away. When they ask what you are doing, say "Well you never know where those hands have been." Or "Don't take it personal, just trying to clean up."

Brothers

B is for the bond that can never be
taken away.

R is for the refuge that you have to
me each day.

O is for the oath that we will always
remain as friends.

T is for the truth upon which
everything depends.

H is for the honor it is to be your
brother.

E is for encouragement that we give
to one another.

R is for the road that we have
traveled down so far.

S is for security, for when I need you,
there you are.

~ Wendy Silva

48. Backatchya

Whenever your sibling says anything – anything at all – point at them and say "Right back atchya sis!" or "Right back at ya bro".

"Ohana means family, family means nobody gets left behind. Or forgotten."

~ Lilo and Stitch

49. Toothbrush

Put your sibling's toothbrush in a different place every now and then. Put it in a place they will not expect, like in the shower, or on their bureau, or in the refrigerator right in plain sight. When they ask why their toothbrush has been moved, you can pretend you don't know what they are talking about and suggest that it must be a sign from the tooth fairy that they need to brush more!

Another fun, yet harmless thing you can do is wet your sibling's toothbrush and shake a little bit of salt on it.

"Your siblings are the only people in the world who know what it's like to have been brought up the way you were."

~ *Betsy Cohen*

50. Mismatched socks

Mix up your siblings socks. If they have a green sock, pair it up with a white one. Pair up his footie socks with knee highs, etc.

"The best thing about having a sister was that I always had a friend."

~ *Cali Rae Turner*

51. Why, why, why

Revert back to when you were four or five years old and anytime your sibling says something, ask "Why?" Just keep repeating that question. "Why?", "But why?" "Why?" It will be funny to see how long it takes for them to figure out that you're just playing with them.

"A family is a clan held together
with the glue of love and the
cement of mutual respect."

~ Unknown

52. Clip-on earrings

Get some inexpensive, yet comfortable clip-on earrings. While your brother is sleeping, put them on him. If you can only get one earring on, that's okay. It will be funny to see his reaction first thing in the morning when he sees himself in the mirror.

"All for one and one for all
My brother and my friend
What fun we have
The time we share
Brothers 'til the end."

~ *Unknown*

53. Sharing

Nonchalantly eat off your sibling's plate or take a sip from their cup. Pretend this is completely normal. When they ask what you are doing, ask, "What? Weren't we always taught that sharing is caring?"

"Family is one of nature's masterpieces."

~ *George Santayana*

54 There's a bug in my soup!

Find some small plastic insects and freeze them in cubes of ice. You can then put them in your sibling's drinks. You can also just toss them into their soup, cereal, etc.

"Each of our lives will always be a special part of the other."

~ *Unknown*

55. Super soaked

Most kitchen sinks have a spray nozzle. Take a rubber band and wrap it around the entire spray nozzle including the trigger. Be sure the water is turned off before doing this or you will spray yourself. Point it in the direction you think it needs to be in. Tell your sibling they should wash their hands before dinner or give them any reason you can think of. Did they blow their nose? Or pet the dog? When they turn on the water to wash their hands they will be sprayed with water.

Have a towel ready for clean up.

"Sisters is probably the most competitive relationship within the family, but once the sisters are grown, it becomes the strongest relationship."

~Margaret Mead

56. Runaway mouse!

Before your sibling goes to use the computer, unplug the mouse in the back of the computer. (Just remember what slot it needs to go back into.) Your brother or sister will not know what is wrong and will try to figure it out. See how long it takes them.

Of course if they have homework they need to get done, don't wait too long before you tell them that the mouse is unplugged. But if they are just surfing the web, you can wait it out. Ha ha.

"We are more than just acquaintances...it's as if we are cut from the same fabric. Even though we appear to be sewn in a different pattern, we have a common thread that won't be broken, by people or years or distance."

~ *Unknown*

57. Who are you?

Put on any mask you can find, a Halloween mask, a clown mask, a ski mask, a toy mask, a fun mask or any wig, scarf and sun glasses. You could even make a mask out of construction paper. As your sibling sleeps get really close to their face, then wait patiently for them to wake up. It will take them a few seconds for their eyes to adjust to what they are seeing but it's a great wake-up call and better then the snooze button. This is good on school days because we guarantee they won't fall back to sleep.

"Like branches on a tree we grow in different directions yet our roots remain as one. Each of our lives will always be a special part of the other."

~ *Unknown*

58. Soft hands

Everyone should have soft hands. Hand lotion helps with that and is harmless on doorknobs. Put hand lotion on the doorknobs that your sibling will be using. You can also put lotion on the handles or knobs to their bureaus as well.

"If you don't understand how a woman could both love her sister dearly and want to wring her neck at the same time, then you were probably an only child."

~ *Linda Sunshine*

59. And they all fall down

Ping pong balls are inexpensive and light. Put several in a medicine cabinet or any cabinet that you know your sibling will be getting into. It's fun to see and hear their reaction as the balls fall out and bounce all over the place.

"Siblings touch your heart in ways no other could. Siblings share everything... their hopes, their fears, their love. Real friendship springs from their special bonds."

~ *Unknown*

60. Lost and found

Take your siblings cell phone and tape it under a chair or desk. Gently wrap it in a paper towel so that tape residue doesn't get on the phone. Once it is securely in place, go around the corner and call it. He or she will never suspect that it is taped under something so it will take them a while to find it.

"There's a special kind of freedom siblings enjoy. Freedom to share innermost thoughts, to ask favors, to show their true feelings. The freedom to simply be themselves."

~ *Unknown*

61. Green bean launch

Food fights really aren't cool because they are way too messy. *But* the green bean launch is mess free and fun. When your sibling is least expecting it, launch a green bean their way. Ha ha ha, this makes us laugh just thinking of it because we've done it before and it's funny!

"Ah siblings, they've been with you for so long they probably know you better than anyone else. Maybe even better than you know yourself."

~*Unknown*

62. Yarn maze

Get some string or yarn. We like to use different colors of yarn. Make sure your sibling will be away for a bit so that you have time to set it up. Tape the yarn from one side of the room to the other. Then crisscross it and do it again and again and again. Tie or tape it to anything you can find or think of. When you're done, you will have a yarn maze that is actually a lot of fun to try to get through, but your sibling will be surprised for sure!

Clean up is fairly easy and takes less time than it did to create it.

"Although I hate to admit it and won't, I miss my siblings when they are away."

~ *Unknown*

63. Name change

When your sibling is in the shower, outside doing chores, or away from their cell phone, take it and change your name in their address book. Change your name to "Mom" or "Dad" or anyone else you'd like to send them a pretend message from. If you change YOUR name to "Dad" in their cell phone address book and send them a text message, they will see it and automatically think it's from Dad. In your text message you can tell them to do YOUR chores. They will think Dad is telling them to do so.

Be sure to clue them in quickly that this is a joke because it's not that cool to touch someone else's phone. BUT it is funny for a few minutes, especially when your sibling starts doing YOUR chores!

There you have it, fun and easy ideas on how to joke with your sibling. If you would like to contact us, either to tell us how these ideas helped create fun, long-lasting memories or to share some of your own ideas please email us at:

prankandprayyougetaway@findyourwaypublishing.com

We look forward to hearing from you!

About the Authors

William Eshleman is an honor student and lives in Maine. He is extremely easy going and brings joy to all he comes in contact with. He enjoys being outdoors, plays soccer and basketball, and participated in competitive diving in Colorado where his mom resides.

Paige Kimball is an honor student and lives in Maine. She has a great sense of humor and makes her family and friends laugh often. She plays the piano and guitar. She likes to travel and her favorite trip was to Paris, France and Germany where she visited her dad, who is in the military. Paige also enjoys reading, swimming, hiking, dancing, biking, and spending time with friends and family.

William and Paige had the idea for this book after using many of them on their brother, Wyatt. They enjoy lovingly teasing Wyatt and their sister, Marrae. Paige and William feel truly blessed to have their siblings in their lives and will always cherish the memories, the laughs, and the love. They have great respect for their siblings and know that Wyatt & Marrae will have great fun trying these ideas on them! They wrote this simple book to help siblings and families create, fun-loving memories to last a lifetime.

Disclaimer

Prank
and
Pray You Get Away!

Over 60 Fun Jokes to Play on Your Sibling

Quick Order Form

Fax orders: 207-514-0438.
Please send this form with your order.

Telephone orders: 207-514-0575

Internet orders:
www.findyourwaypublishing.com

Postal orders:
Find Your Way Publishing, Inc.
PO Box 667
Norway, ME 04268
USA

Please include:

Name of book: _____

Quantity: _____

Your Name: _____

Address: _____

City: _____

State: _____

Zip: _____

Telephone: _____

Email address: _____

Prank
and
Pray You Get Away!

Over 60 Fun Jokes to Play on Your Sibling

Quick Order Form

Fax orders: 207-514-0438.
Please send this form with your order.

Telephone orders: 207-514-0575

Internet orders:
www.findyourwaypublishing.com

Postal orders:
Find Your Way Publishing, Inc.
PO Box 667
Norway, ME 04268
USA

Please include:

Name of book: _____

Quantity: _____

Your Name: _____

Address: _____

City: _____

State: _____

Zip: _____

Telephone: _____

Email address: _____

CPSIA information can be obtained at www.ICGtesting.com
Printed in the USA
BVOW04s1832250115

384879BV00006B/22/P